THIS BOOK BELONG TO

_____

LONDON 2012 OLYMPICS

1. In which sport did the North Korean players walk off the pitch after their images were shown on the screen behind a South Korean flag?

2. How many gold medals did Australia win?
   a. 5   b. 7   c. 9   d. 11

3. Which British broadcaster invented Mo Farah's signature Mo-Bot?

4. Which country's women athletes were made to fly economy to London while the men flew business class?

5. Which country was not able to watch the opening ceremony live on television?
   a. France   b. United Kingdom   c. Germany   d. United States

6. Which British legend officially opened the 'Isles of wonder' opening ceremony by ringing an enormous bell?
   a. Chris Hoy   b. Bradley Wiggins   c. Andy Murray

7. Which famous Brit parachuted into the Olympic stadium as part of the opening ceremony?
   a. James Bond   b. David Cameron   c. The Queen

8. Helen Glover and Heather Stanning won Britain's first gold medals of the games. What sport was this in?

9. Who did Andy Murray beat in the final to win the gold in tennis?

10. What was the name of the London 2012 mascot?

    a. Godrick   b. Wenlock   c. Lucas   d. Goldilocks

11. Which country won the men's football?
    a. Brazil   b. Germany   c. Argentina   d. Mexico

12. Which sport had eight competitors disqualified for 'not using one's best efforts to win'?
    a. Badminton   b. Archery   c. Marathon   d. Judo

13. Which medal did Britain's Tom Daley win?
    a. Gold   b. Silver   c. Bronze   d. None

14. Who ended the closing ceremony?
    a. Pink Floyd   b. The Who   c. Queen   d. Rolling Stones

15. Who smashed the world record to win the men's 800m?
    a. David Rudisha   b. Andrew Osagie   c. Mohammad Aman

OLYMPIC RECORDS

Across

3. Who set the record for shot put at the 2016 Olympics with the first name Ryan?
5. Who holds the record for the women's 100m?
7. What country is Tiki Gelana from who set the women's marathon record in 2012?
8. What American female swimmer holds the record for the 200m freestyle that was set in 2012?
10. Which U.S athlete with the first name Bob set the long jump world record of 8.9m in 1968?
12. Which country has won gold at the football the most times in the Olympics?
15. What country is David Rudisha from who set the 800m Olympic record at the 2012 Olympics?
16. Who holds the record for the most singles gold medals in men's tennis?

Down

1. Since 1988 China has won a staggering 41 gold medals in table tennis. How many golds have been won by non-Chinese Olympians?
2. Who holds the record for the men's 200m with a time of 19.30?
4. Who holds the record for the men's 100m freestyle that was set in 2008?
6. Ian Miller holds the record for the most appearances at the Olympics with 10. What sport has Miller achieved this in?
9. Which male cyclist set the record for the 1km time trial in 2004?
11. Who holds the record for the most gold medals in women's tennis?
13. To the nearest 10m how far is the Olympic record for javelin?
14. What British male set the record for the 100m breaststroke in 2016?

USAIN BOLT

1. Before specialising in sprinting, what other sport did Bolt excel in?

2. How tall is Usain Bolt?
   a. 6 feet 3   b. 6 feet 4   c. 6 feet 5   d. 6 feet 6

3. Which of the following has Bolt not set a world record in?
   a. 100m   b. 200m   c. 400m   d. 4x100m relay

4. What is Usain Bolt's fastest 100m?

5. What is the name of Bolt's main running coach?
   a. Thompson   b. Campbell   c. Bowerman   d. Mills

6. Why did Bolt not win gold in the 100m at the 2011 world championships?

7. Which British football team does Bolt support?

8. Which British athlete did Usain Bolt pay tribute to at London 2012, by impersonating their signature pose?

9. Bolt's rise to stardom came at the 2008 Beijing Olympics. How many medals did he win at this games?

10. At the Olympic Games of 2008 in Beijing, Bolt dined on which 'delicacy' before his races?

    a. Chicken nuggets   b. Cheese burger   c. Ice cream

11. In what country on August 16, 2009, did Usain set a world record for the 100m and 200m?

12. What is Bolt's unusual middle name?

    a. Yaquareo   b. St Patrick   c. Lighting   d. St Leo

13. How old was Bolt when he turned professional?

14. True or false: Bolt turned down several scholarships to American colleges.

15. In what year was Usain Bolt born?

    a. 1986   b. 1984   c. 1988   d. 1989

16. In what year did Bolt make his Olympic debut?

17. How many sub 10 second 100m has Bolt ran?

    a. 30   b. 36   c. 43   d. 50

18. How many world championship medals has Bolt won during his career?

    a. 13   b. 15   c. 17   d. 20

I KNOW
WHAT I CAN DO,
SO, I NEVER
DOUBT MYSELF
–USAIN BOLT

HISTORY OF THE OLYMPICS

Across
1. What are Olympic gold medals mostly made of?
5. Where was the first modern Olympic games held?
6. What was the first team sport to be added to the Olympics?
8. The five rings represent the five different inhabited _____ of the world.
11. The first black athlete to compete at the Olympics was from which country?
13. How many times have the Olympics been held in South America?
14. In ancient times, where were the Olympics held?
15. In what decade did it become illegal for Olympic athletes to use performance enhancing drugs?
16. There are always three official languages at an Olympic games: the host language, English and what else?

Down
2. In which century BC did the Olympic games begin?
3. Which sport in the ancient Olympic games allowed finger breaking?
4. The 2012 Olympics was the first Olympics where every country sent female athletes. Where was this Olympics held?
7. At which Olympics did a tragic massacre occur in 1972?
9. In which century were women allowed to compete at the Olympics?
10. Which US city was the first to host the modern Olympics?
12. The torch relay made its debut at the 1936 Olympic games. Where was this Olympics held?

GUESS THE ATHLETE

1. This athlete has won 9 Olympic gold medals, and 10 world championship medals. His career spanned from 1979-1996 when he won his last Olympic event.

2. This Romanian gymnast is a five-time Olympic gold medallist and was born in 1961.

3. This American female has won six Olympic gold medals. She is a track and field sprinter and was born in 1985.

4. This woman is the first swimmer to represent the United States in five Olympic games, and at 41 years old, the oldest swimmer to earn a place on the U.S Olympic team.

5. This male gymnast was born in 1976 and is one of the most decorated gymnasts of all time. He has won 12 Olympic medals and five world championships.

6. This athlete won the tennis gold medal at the 2008 Beijing Olympics.

7. This player captained Brazil to victory over Germany at the 2016 Olympics in football.

8. This American sprinter won four gold medals and was born in 1967. He is 6 feet 1 and is the only male athlete to win both the 200 and 400m event at the same Olympics.

9. This sprinter became the youngest 100m winner of all time at the 2011 world championships.

10. This Finish runner was born in 1949 and won four gold medals at the 1972 and 1976 Olympic games.

11. This female tennis player has won four Olympic golds, with two coming at the 2012 London Olympic games.

12. This man has won one Olympic gold and one world championships in long jump and was a champion of the British TV show MasterChef in 2019.

13. This Jamaican woman won gold at the 2016 Olympics 100m with a time of 10.71.

14. This Brit won gold at the 2016 Olympics in golf who is born in 1980.

15. Which British female with a very tough name to spell won gold in the 400m at the 2008 Olympics? She has an MBE and was born in 1984.

MICHAEL PHELPS

Across

3. How many inches over 6 foot is Phelps' arm span?
6. During the 2008 Beijing Olympics Phelps set the record for the most gold records at a games. How many golds did he win?
7. Phelps became the youngest man to ever set a swimming world record. How many years old was he when he achieved this?
9. At the 2004 Athens Olympics, Phelps set seven records. How many of those were world records?
10. What does Phelps say is his worst stroke?
11. Complete Phelps' nickname: the Baltimore _____
13. Which stroke is Michael Phelps' signature stroke?
14. What is Phelps' hometown?
16. Which company awarded Phelps with a $1 million bonus after breaking the gold medal record?

Down

1. How many medals has Phelps won at the Olympics that were not golds?
2. Without Phelps at the 2004 Olympics, the USA would not have won on overall gold medals. Who would have overtaken them?
3. Who held the previous record for most gold medals at a single Olympic games before Phelps?
4. How many gold medals does Michael Phelps have?
5. How many more gold medals has Phelps won than Usain Bolt?
8. How many swimming caps does Phelps wear when racing?
12. Where were Michael Phelps first Olympics held?
15. Which disorder was Phelps diagnosed with as a child?
16. At the 2004 Olympics in Athens, how many gold medals did Phelps win?

IF YOU WANT TO
BE THE BEST,
YOU HAVE TO DO
THINGS THAT OTHER
PEOPLE AREN'T
WILLING TO DO
—MICHAEL PHELPS

GENERAL KNOWLEDGE

1. What are the colours of the five interlaced rings in the Olympic flag?

2. _____ refers to a four-year period beginning on the opening of the Olympic Games for the summer sports.

3. Which sport was included in the 1988 Olympics after a break of 64 years?

4. How many Spanish athletes have won gold at the winter Olympic games?
   a. 0   b. 1   c. 2   d. 3

5. In which year was Snowboarding was first included in the Winter Olympics in Nagano, Japan?

6. In 1980 Moscow Olympics one country boycotted the games with the order of its President. Which was that country?
   a. United Kingdom   b. Germany   c. United States   d. France

7. _____ was a female skater who had was a three-time Olympic Champion in Ladies' Singles, a ten-time World Champion and a six-time European Champion.

8. Name the country which always leads the parade of athletes at the Olympic opening ceremony?

9. Which country in 1992 Summer Olympics Barcelona, Spain was allowed to compete in the Olympic Games for the first time since the 1960 Summer Olympics, after a long suspension for its apartheid policy?

10. There was a mass boycotting of one of the Olympic Games where 64 countries opted to miss it. What year was this?

   a. 1972   b. 1964   c. 1980   d. 1988

11. There have been two Olympic Games in which South Korea and North Korea have come together under one flag. One was in 2018, but when was the other one?

   a. 2000   b. 1996   c. 1992   d. 2012

12. As a symbol of spreading peace, which bird is set free during the inaugural ceremony of Olympic Games?

13. The first World War cancelled one Olympics which was planned to be held at _____ in 1916

14. Oliver Kirk won 2 gold medals at the same Olympics in boxing in 1904. What makes his two golds special, and a record that still stands today?

15. Badminton was declared as an event from which Olympics?

   a. 1952   b. 1968   c. 1980   d. 1992

OLYMPIC SPORTS

Across

3. Finish the Olympic swimming event: 200m Individual _____.
6. What sport is set to be introduced at the Tokyo 2021 Olympics which involves handholds?
8. At the diving in the Olympics there are two events. One is the 10m Platform, but what is the 3m dive called?
10. What sport is set to be introduced at the Tokyo 2021 Olympics, that takes place on water?
12. What is the race called where the runners jump over fences and land in water?
13. What event is only performed by women and was introduced at the 1952 Olympics?
14. At the first modern Olympics there were two sports starting with S. One was swimming but what was the other one?
16. What sport is set to be introduced at the Tokyo 2021 Olympics that is big in America?

Down

1. At the first Olympics where women could compete, they only did so in two events. One was golf but what was the other?
2. What sport beginning with F was present at the first modern Olympics?
4. What type of event is the men's 50km ____?
5. There are 4 throwing events at the Olympics: Javelin, Discus, Shot Put and what else?
7. What sport was introduced at the 2000 Olympics and starts with T?
9. Finish the Olympic event that is only performed by men: _____ horse.
11. Men at the Olympics do the decathlon, but what is the women's equivalent?
15. What sport is known as _____ slalom that is not on a ski slope?

15

GUESS THE YEAR

1. What year did Chris Hoy win his first gold medal?

    a. 2000   b. 2004   c. 2008   d. 2012

2. What year did Maurice Greene win the 100m gold medal?

    a. 1988   b. 1992   c. 1996   d. 2000

3. Gail Devers was only the second woman to defend her 100m title at the Olympics. What year did she first win it?

    a. 1992   b. 1996   c. 2000   d. 2008

4. What year did Mo Farah win his first Olympic gold medal?

    a. 2004   b. 2008   c. 2012   d. 2016

5. What year did Jemima Sumgong win the women's marathon at the Olympics?

    a. 2016   b. 2012   c. 2004   d. 1992

6. What year did Linford Christie win his first 100m Olympic gold medal?

    a. 1984   b. 1988   c. 1992   d. 2000

7. Sir Steve Redgrave won Olympic gold medals at five consecutive Olympic games. In what year did he win his last Olympic gold?

a. 2008   b. 2000   c. 1992   d. 1988

8. In what year did Natalie Coughlin become the first U.S. female athlete in modern Olympic history to win six medals in one Olympiad?

   a. 2000   b. 2008   c. 2012   d. 2016

9. Paavo Nurmi (also known as the flying Finn) won nine gold medals and three silver medals and went unbeaten for an unprecedented 121 races. In what year did he win his last Olympic gold?

   a. 1904   b. 1912   c. 1920   d. 1928

10. What year did Carl Lewis win the last of his eight gold medals?

    a. 1968   b. 1960   c. 1982   d. 1996

11. What year did Nicola Adams win her only gold medal?

    a. 2016   b. 2012   c. 2008   d. 2000

12. What year did Great Britain come second in the overall gold medal standings with 27 golds, finishing one above China?

    a. 2016   b. 2012   c. 2008   d. 2004

13. In what year did the Soviet Union boycott the Olympic games, which is believed to be in response to many nations boycotting the Moscow games 4 years earlier?

a. 1976   b. 1980   c. 1984   d. 1988

14. In what year was Ben Johnson stripped of his 100m gold medal due to a failed drug test after the games?

a. 1972   b. 1968   c. 1980   d. 1988

15. In what year did Dong Fangxiao lie about her age in the gymnastics claiming that she was 16 when she was in fact 14?

a. 2000   b. 2004   c. 2008   d. 2012

WINTER OLYMPICS

Across

2. In which French city were the first winter Olympics in 1924 held?
8. How many countries in the southern hemisphere have hosted the winter Olympics?
9. What was the famous skier Hermann Maier's nickname?
10. What is the name of the Norwegian cross-country skier who is the most decorated winter Olympian (8 golds, 4 silver, 3 bronze)?
13. What country hosted the 2018 winter Olympics?
14. In which city were the 2010 winter Olympics hosted?
16. What is the most successful nation at the winter Olympics?

Down

1. Which multiple Oscar winner did the opening and closing ceremony at the 1960 winter Olympics?
3. Australia and what other country are the only two south of the equator that have medalled at the winter Olympics?
4. What was the nickname for the famously hopeless British skier named Eddie Edwards?
5. One of the biggest Olympic scandals occurred at the 2002 games where both Canada and Russia shared gold. What sport was this in?
6. What Austrian city has hosted the winter Olympics twice?
7. Which American speed skater won all five gold medals at the 1980 Lake Placid games?
11. What is the only country to have won gold at every winter Olympics?
12. At the 1984 Olympic games Dean and _____ became the highest scoring figure skaters of all time achieving a perfect score.
15. What is the only European capital city to have hosted the winter Olympics?

WINTER OLYMPICS RECORDS

1. How old was America's Chloe Kim when she became the youngest female snowboarding gold medallist in 2018?

    a. 15   b. 16   c. 17   d. 18

2. Jocelyne Lamoureux-Davidson made back-to-back goals in a blazing six seconds in the ice hockey at the 2018 Olympics setting the record for quickest back to back goals. What country does she play for?

3. Who holds the record for the most snowboarding gold medals with three?

4. How old was Axsel Svindal when he became the oldest skiing gold medallist in 2018?

    a. 31   b. 32   c. 34   d. 35

5. Noriaki Kasai holds the records for the most winter Olympic appearances for an athlete. What sport is this in?

    a. Downhill skiing   b. Ski Jumping   c. Biathlon

6. What is the name of the Russian figure skater who won gold at the 2018 winter Olympics? Being only 15 years old, she set the record for the highest figure skating score ever

7. Which event at the winter Olympics has the most gold medals on offer?

    a. Biathlon   b. Alpine skiing   c. Figure skating   d. Speed skating

8. The United States are second on the list for all time gold medals won, and have won 305 medals over the 23 games they have competed in. How many of these were gold?

   a. 85   b. 90   c. 95   d. 105

9. At the 2018 Olympics this athlete unbelievably managed to win the snowboarding parallel giant slalom, before borrowing the skis off another competitor to win gold at the Super-G. What was her name?

10. Which country has hosted the winter Olympics the most times with four?

11. Norway set the record at the 2018 Olympics for the most medals at a single games (39). How many of these were gold?

   a. 10   b. 14   c. 16   d. 18

12. Which male ski jumper holds the record for the most Olympic gold medals?

13. Which country holds the record for the most skiing gold medals?

   a. Austria   b. Switzerland   c. France   d. Germany

14. How many gold medals have Scott Moir and Tessa Virtue won in figure skating, making them the most decorated Olympic skaters of all time?

   a. 2   b. 3   c. 4   d. 5

15. Which country has won the most gold medals in ice hockey at the winter Olympics?

BRITISH OLYMPIANS

Across
4. Great Britain's first gold medal in the Beijing Olympics was their 200th in the modern games. It was also the first for which British country for 36 years?
5. How many gold medals has the sailor Ben Ainslie won?
8. Linford Christie won gold in the 100m at the 1992 Olympics, but what country was he born in?
10. In 2012, which female cyclist got disqualified in the semi-finals of the women's team sprint, only to win gold the day after?
11. Sir Chris Hoy and what other British Olympian are Britain's most decorated athletes?
14. In what place did silver medallist Linford Christie cross the finish line in the 100 metres at the Seoul Olympics in 1988?
15. Less than two weeks after becoming the first Briton to win the Tour de France, this cyclist won an Olympic gold medal in 2012.

Down
1. Which British swimmer won the 200m breaststroke in 1976, stopping USA from winning every swimming event?
2. Which British sprinter won gold in the 100m in 1924, inspiring the movie 'Chariots of Fire'?
3. Sean Kerly, Imran Sherwani and Ian Taylor were all members of Great Britain's gold-medal winning team in the 1988 Olympics. What sport was this in?
6. What colour medal did Amir Khan win at the 2004 Olympic games?
7. What British male won gold in the 100m breaststroke at the 1980 Olympic games?
9. Which British princess represented Great Britain at the 1976 games?
12. Who won gold in the 2012 heptathlon?
13. In what sport did Nicola Adams become the first ever woman to win gold at the 2012 Olympic games?

GUESS THE WINTER OLYMPICS

1. Where were the winter Olympics in 2018?
2. Where were the winter Olympics in 1998?
3. Where were the winter Olympics in 1988?
4. Where were the winter Olympics in 2006?
5. Where were the winter Olympics in 1928?
6. Where were the winter Olympics in 2014?
7. Where were the winter Olympics in 2002?
8. Where were the winter Olympics in 1976?
9. Where were the winter Olympics in 2010?
10. Where were the winter Olympics in 1994?
11. Where were the winter Olympics in 1936?
12. Where were the winter Olympics in 1948?
13. Where were the winter Olympics in 1992?
14. Where were the winter Olympics in 1980?
15. Where were the winter Olympics in 1968?

GUESS THE SUMMER OLYMPICS

Across
4. Where were the Olympics in 1900?
5. Where were the Olympics in 1976?
9. Where were the Olympics in 1948?
10. Where were the Olympics in 1896?
11. Where will the Olympics be in 2024?
12. Where were the Olympics in 1952?
13. Where were the Olympics in 1988?
15. Where will the Olympics be in 2028?
16. Where were the Olympics in 1968?

Down
1. Where were the Olympics in 2016?
2. Where will the Olympics be in 2021?
3. Where were the Olympics in 1992?
6. Where were the Olympics in 2000?
7. Where were the Olympics in 1936?
8. Where were the Olympics in 1996?
14. Where were the Olympics in 1920?

RIO 2016 OLYMPICS

1. Usain Bolt made Olympic history winning his third consecutive gold in the men's 100m. What was his time?
   a. 9.81   b. 9.68   c. 9.89   d. 9.75

2. Swimmer Cate Campbell called one of her swims "possibly the greatest choke in Olympic history". What race was she talking about?

3. Chloe Esposito won Australia's first ever medal in the modern pentathlon when she claimed gold. In what place did she start the final round?
   a. 3rd   b. 5th   c. 7th   d. 9th

4. How many gold medals did Simone Biles win, equalling the gymnastics record?
   a. 3   b. 4   c. 5   d. 6

5. What was the score at the end of regular time in the final of the football?
   a. 0-0   b. 1-1   c. 2-2   d. 3-3

6. Vinicius was the official _____ of the 2016 Rio Summer Olympics.
   a. Logo   b. Motto   c. Mascot

7. Which sports were included in the 2016 Rio Olympics for the first time in many years?

a. Golf and Football   b. Golf and BMX   c. Rugby and Cricket

8. What sport was held at the velodrome?

9. How many gold medals did the USA win overall at the game, put them at number one at the 2016 Olympics?
   a. 32   b. 37   c. 42   d. 46

10. What is the name of the virus that raised fears regarding its potential impact on athletes and visitors?

11. What Asian country starting with T won their first ever medal?

12. How many different events were there at the Rio Olympics?
    a. 306   b. 212   c. 404   d. 365

13. Which of the following countries sent athletes to the 2016 Olympics for the first time in their history?
    a. Bermuda   b. South Sudan   c. Kosovo   d. Gabon

14. Jason Kenny and his fiancée Laura Trott both claimed cycling gold medals. How many medals have they got combined?
    a. 8   b. 9   c. 10   d. 11

15. Shaunae Miller became a meme after launching herself across the line to win which event?
    a. 100m   b. 200m   c. 400m   d. 800m

ANSWERS

LONDON 2012 OLYMPICS

1. Football
2. 7
3. Clare Balding
4. Japan
5. United States
6. Bradley Wiggins
7. The queen
8. Rowing
9. Roger Federer
10. Wenlock
11. Mexico
12. Badminton
13. Bronze
14. The Who
15. David Rudisha

OLYMPIC RECORDS

USAIN BOLT QUIZ

1. Cricket
2. 6 feet 5
3. 400m
4. 9.58
5. Mills
6. He was disqualified for a false start.
7. Manchester United
8. Mo Farah
9. Three
10. Chicken nuggets
11. Germany
12. St Leo
13. 18
14. True
15. 1986
16. 2004
17. 50
18. 13

HISTORY OF THE OLYMPICS

GUESS THE ATHLETE QUIZ

1. Carl Lewis
2. Nadia Comaneci
3. Allyson Felix
4. Dara Torres
5. Alexei Nemov
6. Rafael Nadal
7. Neymar
8. Michael Johnson
9. Yohan Blake
10. Lasse Viren
11. Serena Williams
12. Greg Rutherford
13. Shelly-Ann Fraser-Pryce
14. Justin Rose
15. Christine Ohuruogu

MICHAEL PHELPS

GENERAL KNOWLEDGE

1. Red, Black, Breen, Blue and Yellow

2. Olympiad

3. Tennis

4. One

5. 1998

6. United States

7. Sonja Henie

8. Greece

9. South Africa

10. 1980

11. 2000

12. Dove

13. Berlin

14. He won them in two different events (different weight categories)

15. 1992

OLYMPIC SPORTS

GUESS THE YEAR QUIZ

1. 2004
2. 2000
3. 1992
4. 2012
5. 2016
6. 1992
7. 2000
8. 2008
9. 1928
10. 1996
11. 2016
12. 2016
13. 1984
14. 1988
15. 2000

WINTER OLYMPICS

	W														
C	H	A	M	O	N	I	X								
	A	L			E										
		T			W										
		D			Z		T		F				H		
		I			E		H		I		I		Z	E	R	O
		S			A		E		G		N		E		
		N			L		E		U		N		I		
	H	E	R	M	A	N	N	A	T	O	R		D		
		Y			N		G		E		B	J	O	R	G	E	N
					D		L		S		R		N	
							E		K		U		U	
						T			A		C		S	
				S	O	U	T	H	K	O	R	E	A	
						R			T					
						V	A	N	C	O	U	V	E	R
						I			G		S			
						L					L			
						L			N	O	R	W	A	Y

WINTER OLYMPIC RECORDS QUIZ

1. 17
2. USA
3. Shaun White
4. 35
5. Ski jumping
6. Alina Zagitova
7. Speed Skating
8. 105
9. Ester Ledecká
10. USA
11. 14
12. Simon Ammann
13. Austria
14. 3
15. Canada

BRITISH OLYMPIANS

```
                                    W
                                    I
                          A         L
                          B         K
                          R         I
              H       W   A   L   E   S
        F   O   U   R     H
            C         S   A
            K         I   G       J   A   M   A   I   C   A
        P   E   N   D   L   E   T   O   N               N
            Y         V   O                   K   E   N   N   Y
                      E   D       B           N       E
        T   H   I   R   D       O           N
                          H       X           I
                          E   W   I   G   G   I   N   S
                          N
                          G
```

GUESS THE WINTER OLYMPICS

1. South Korea
2. Japan
3. Canada
4. Italy
5. Switzerland
6. Russia
7. United States
8. Austria
9. Canada
10. Norway
11. Germany
12. Switzerland
13. France
14. United States
15. France

GUESS THE OLYMPICS

RIO 2016 OLYMPICS

1. 9.81
2. 100m freestyle
3. 7th
4. 4
5. 1-1
6. Mascot
7. Golf and football
8. Cycling
9. 46
10. Zika Virus
11. Tajikistan
12. 306
13. South Sudan
14. 11
15. 400m

Printed in Great Britain
by Amazon